We Help at School

Craig Rose

ROSEN
COMMON CORE
READERS

Rosen Classroom™

New York

Published in 2013 by The Rosen Publishing Group, Inc.
29 East 21st Street, New York, NY 10010

Book Design: Michael Harmon

Photo Credits: Cover Darrin Henry/Shutterstock.com; p. 5 Yellow Dog Productions/Lifesize/Getty Images;
p. 7 Vitaly Titov & Maria Sidelnikova/Shutterstock.com; p. 9 © iStockphoto.com/A330Pilot;
p. 11 Regine Mahaux/The Image Bank/Getty Images; p. 13 © iStockphoto.com/gmnicholas;
p. 15 © iStockphoto.com/AISPIX.

ISBN: 978-1-4488-8661-6
6-pack ISBN: 978-1-4488-8667-8

Manufactured in the United States of America

CPSIA Compliance Information: Batch #WS12RC: For further information contact Rosen Publishing, New York, New York at 1-800-237-9932.

Word Count: 24

Contents

We help at school.

Grace cleans the desk.

Logan opens the door.

2

Katie waters the plant.

Tim feeds the fish.

13

Claire picks up toys.

Words to Know

desk

door

fish

plant

Index